Shall I go to war With my American Brethren? A Discourse From Judges the Xxth and 28th. Addressed to all Concerned in Determining That Important Question

A

D I S C O U R S E

FROM

J U D G E S xx. 28.

[Price One Shilling.]

SHALL I GO TO WAR WITH MY
AMERICAN BRETHREN?

A

DISCOURSE

FROM

JUDGES the xxth and 28th.

Addreſſed to A L L concerned in determining

THAT IMPORTANT QUESTION.

LONDON:

Printed for G. KEARSLY, at Nº 1, Ludgate-ſtreet.

MDCCLXIX.

JUDGES xx. 28.

Shall I yet again go out to battle againſt the children of Benjamin my bròther, or ſhall I ceaſe?

IF the denomination of Chriſtians to which I belong, and my rank in the church, gave me the honour of ad-dreſſing you from the pulpit, I ſhould re-member, that my buſineſs there was not to diſcuſs political queſtions, and to deter-mine the diſputed rights of ſovereigns and ſubjects, but to explain and inculcate the great truths and duties of our holy reli-gion; and among theſe I would not fail warmly to recommend, loyalty to our prince, love to our country, and a willing-neſs to ſacrifice pleaſure, eaſe, wealth, and preferment, to the public good. But the ſciences are not, as trade and manufactures, confined to particular corporations. If

B   men

men make confcience of the public and private duties of the offices with which they are invefted, it is lawful, nay, on fome occafions, it is laudable, in their leifure hours, to unbend their minds by a change of ftudy, to follow where their genius leads them, and to impart their thoughts to the public, if they fee caufe. The exercife of government, and the authoritatively deciding political queftions, muft be the work of the few; but to ftudy politics, and to write of them, is the right of every free-born Briton. Every Chriftian may afpire after the blefling of the peacemaker. One who has a mean rank in a family, one who has no rank in it at all, is authorifed, is obliged, if he fees a houfe on flames, to call upon thofe who may have it in their power to extinguifh them. My duty as a Minifter does not annihilate my duty to the beft of Princes, and to my dear fellow fubjects. If a watchman fee danger approaching, and blow not the trumpet, the blood of the people, whom he neglected to warn, fhall be required at his hand. If we

forbear

forbear to deliver them that are drawn unto death, and thofe that are ready to be flain; if we fay, behold, we knew it not; doth not he that pondereth the heart, confider it? and he that keepeth our fouls, doth not he know it? and fhall he not render to every man according to his works? Shall I then, can I with fafety be filent, when my King and Country appear to me in the moft imminent danger?

I love and refpect my Sovereign, not only as the guardian of our civil and religious privileges, but as one, whofe virtues would honour and enoble even a private ftation. I love my country, and I love the pofterity of thofe brave and good men, who fled from the rod of oppreffion in their native land, to what was then a wafte and howling wildernefs; but what now is, and I pray God may ever remain, a fruitful field, a feat of Liberty and of true Religion. The principles of humanity and univerfal benevolence, and the warm attachment I feel to Britifh Liberty, and to the fucceffion in the illuftrious houfe of Hanover, conftrain me,

B 2 though

though it may offend many whom I would not willingly difoblige, to found an alarm. The prudent, I know, will keep filent in fuch a day, for it is an evil day. But a flame, not to fay a difpute between B——n and her Colonies, appears to me in fo alarming a point of view, that I cannot be eafy, without making this feeble effort to prevent it.

If I had opportunity to addrefs our friends on the other fide of the ocean, my beft endeavours fhould be exerted to footh and foften their inflamed minds. I would befeech them to reflect, whether they are able with ten thoufand to meet thofe who come againft them with twenty thoufand? and if it is prudent to run themfelves into greater calamities, by purfuing improper meafures for their relief from leffer grievances? I would tell them, it is madnefs to flatter themfelves, they can form their own terms, however reafonable they think them, from a country fo fuperior to them in wealth and power, or fhun B——n's prefcribing terms to them, however un-

reafonable

reafonable thefe terms may feem to Americans. I would afk, where are their fhips
of war? their brave, experienced, and
well-difciplined army? or where their money and credit, to enable them to make
head againft their mother country? If
they cannot tell me where; if the B——fh
fleet can eafily ruin their trade, lay in
afhes their fea-port towns, and when their
prefent military ftores are exhaufted, hin-
der their obtaining any fufficient recruit of
more: I would intreat them, to prefer a
leffer evil to a greater; and, while their
provoked brethren have not yet drawn the
fword, to fend an embaffy, and defire con-
ditions of peace. I hope, it would be un-
neceffary to caution them againft calling
in the aid of arbitrary bigotted popifh
princes, ambitious of univerfal monarchy,
declared enemies, and often open perfe-
cutors of the Proteftant faith. Surely they
will never commit to fuch hands the defence of their religion and liberties. Thefe
are indeed their worft enemies. But while
they remain under the protection of B—n,
their

their danger even from them, and their charge in defending themfelves, will be inconfiderable.

But what I have now in view, is fomething for undeceiving Gentlemen at home, who have honeftly at heart the public good, and whofe opinion, or influence, may any how contribute to decide the important queftion now in agitation.

And furely the queftion, Shall we go to war with our American Brethren, or fhall we not? is too important to be determined, without afking counfel from above, and in dependance on divine direction, hearkening to the dictates of humanity, of love to our remote fellow-fubjects, of juftice and equity, and of prudent regard to the honour and intereft of prince, parliament, and mother country. Let not truth be defpifed, though it comes to you in a rude unpolifhed ftyle. It was my fortune to be educated at a time, when the ftudy of writing Englifh with correctnefs and propriety, was not cultivated with the diligence

gence with which it now is, and which it well merits.

It muſt be unavoidable neceſſity, and no light and trivial matter, that can warrant our involving any part of mankind in the calamities of war. One who has the leaſt feeling of humanity cannot reflect, without pain, on the deſolation, oppreſſion, and cruelty, to which it unavoidably expoſes many worthy individuals, and virtuous families : and cannot behold, without horror, the outrages committed by the ſons of violence, not only in the heat of a battle, or hurry of a purſuit, but even in cool blood. Murders and rapes are committed with impunity : for they who have power and inclination to puniſh, know it not ; and they who ſee it, dare not complain. The fruitful field, once beautiful as the garden of Eden, is trodden down, and becomes as a waſte and barren wilderneſs. Pleaſant villages, flouriſhing cities, and magnificent palaces, are laid in ruins. Joy is withered away from the ſons of men. The moſt ſuccefsful warrior, as a deſtroy-

ing

ing angel, is the rod of God's indignation
to a guilty world. The garments of the
conquering, as well as of the conquered
nation, are dyed in blood, and in the tri‑
umphant city is heard the voice of lamen-
tation : the wife weeping for her hufband,
and the mother foɪ her children, and re‑
fuſing to be comforted, becauſe they are
not. Surely, ɪf divine vengeance purſues
the murderer of one man, it muſt fall on
thoſe with double weight, who wantonly
occaſion the death of thouſands, and the
miſery of thouſands more.

Befides all this, when war commences,
the fageſt politician cannot foretel who
ſhall triumph. The battle is not always
either to the many or to the ſtrong, but
time and chance happen to all men. Suc-
ceſs or diſappointment depend upon a va-
riety of incidents, which no human wiſ-
dom can foreſee or prevent. The righte-
ous cauſe does not always prevail. An in-
viſible arm dire
ts events in a manner quite
oppoſite to every previous probability ; and
he that putteth on the harneſs in the moſt

2   favourable

favourable circumſtances, hath no reaſon to boaſt himſelf, as though he put it off.

When, therefore, different nations begin to diſcover oppoſite inclinations, to puſh oppoſite intereſts, and to make demands upon one another, about which they are not like to agree; it is prudent cooly to weigh what the event may prove, if matters ſhould come to an extremity; and whether the certain advantages of peace, though it coſt the yielding ſomething we might juſtly claim, do not more than ballance the uncertain advantages of war, advantages not to be purchaſed without great expence of blood and treaſure. A breach once made, of courſe grows wider and wider. Solomon was ſenſible of this. "The beginning of ſtrife," ſays he, "is as the letting out of waters, there-"fore leave off contention, before it be "meddled with." And again, "In the "multitude of counſel there is ſafety, and "with good advice make war."

If war with foreign nations is undeſireable, how ſhocking is it to think of war

C   with

with our own countrymen, connected with us by birth, alliance, or commercial intereft, fo that we cannot hurt them without injuring ourfelves. Shall the friend, the brother, the father, the fon, imbrue their hands in the blood of men, by the tyes of nature, efteem, or gratitude, dear to them as their own fouls? The fancied voice of loyalty or of liberty, calls their refpective votaries to rufh on, and to rifque the confequences, while natural affection whifpers in the breaft, " Let not the mo-
" ther-country forget her children, let not
" the children tear in pieces the bowels of
" the mother. If the child muft be facri-
" ficed, let it be by a favage Indian, or a
" perfidious Frenchman. Let it not be
" by a parent's hand. Let not Abraham's
" trial be our choice."

And what is it, that in fome has well nigh extinguifhed parental compaffion? Whence is it, that they can talk with all imaginable coolnefs, of bombarding the cities of their children, nay, of bringing them to a fcaffold? It is for claims, which

B (befides

(befides a plaufible foundation in charters, the validity of which parliaments and courts of law have ratified, by judging and determining according to them,) are fupported by more than a hundred and thirty years uninterrupted and undifputed poffeffion. In the opinion of Mr. David Hume, whofe authority fome of you too much regard, Britain, before the late glorious Revolution, had no fuch claim as this, for either her civil or her religious liberties. Do we think our forefathers erred, in deeming a claim fufficient, that had a feeble legal fupport? Do we wifh, they had thought and acted otherwife? Have we fuch flavifh, daftardly fpirits, that we would have thought or acted otherwife in their fituation? If we difclaim the charge, let us not be fo uncharitable as to do to others what we would not fhould be done to us.

Should the colonies acknowledge a power in the Britifh parliament to tax them, whatever confidence they may have in the wifdom and moderation of the prefent par-

liament,

liament, it is natural to dread, that in procefs of time, an unequal and difproportionate burden may be laid on their eftates and commerce, to leffen the burden on thofe of the impofers. Plead not, that the colonies being a part of the Britifh empire, a Britifh parliament will naturally confult their welfare, and take as tender a care of their concerns, as of any other part of it. That would be a good argument, if members of parliament, by their property in Britain, had not an intereft diftinct from, and fometimes oppofite to that of the colonies. But as they have fuch a feparate intereft, it muft ftrongly tempt them, in raifing funds for the fuppoit of government, to prefei their own eafe to that of the North Americans. The prefent pai-liament, however willing, can give no fecurity, that the power of taxing fhall not be thus abufed, becaufe no rules or limitations fixed by them, can reftrain fubfequent parliaments from fufpending or alteiing thefe iules, when they judge it for the intereft of the Britifh empiie, and from conduct-

conducting themfelves according to thefe new emergencies, which in their apprehenfions may require new laws, new meafures of government, and new plans of procedure in the exercife of their acknowledged powers.

Though Britons in general are convinced, that the claims of our colonies are not founded either in law or in equity ; yet as thefe claims are not without fpecious pleas, it merits ferious deliberation, whether the conftraining them to renounce them, may not have worfe confequences, than conniving at them. It had need to be fomething highly valuable that we wreft from a foolifh and headftrong child, or an ill-advifed friend, at the hazard of a leg or arm, not to fay of their life. Let us excufe our Am——n Brethren, if an honeft zeal againft what they deem perhaps unreafonable, an encroachment on their natural and unalienable rights, tranfported fome of the more undifceining among them beyond the bounds of decency, and led them to fay and do what, upon reflection,

tion, they muft needs repent. Where is the age, where the country, in which any remarkable efforts for the public good, a-gainft the inroads of real or imagined def-potifm, have been conducted with entire prudence, and no unjuftifiable violence committed in the caufe of liberty ?

But if you difregard the evils in which you may involve our colonies, at leaft re-gard thofe in which B——n herfelf may be involved. If fhe fhould not prevail, how dreadful muft be the confequence ? Our once happy ifland fhall lament, when too late, the ruin of her commerce and naval power, and fee herfelf an eafy prey to her deadly foes.

Tell me not, that it is certain, from the wealth and power of Great Britain, that fhe muft prevail, and that her colonies are as yet too weak to give her any effectual oppofition. That this is probable, I al-low : that it is certain, no wife or modeft man will venture to affert. However we exceed them in number, we would do well to remember, that the New Englanders,

inured

inured from their infancy to fatigue and hardfhip, though unable to face a Britifh army in a fair and open field, may yet be the deftruction of thofe, whofe education was more foft and delicate, by harraffing them with conftant marches, and obliging them to be expofed to the open air in the moft cold and tempeftuous weather. Animated by a fpirit of patriotifm, or of revenge, one has chafed a hundred, and two have put a thoufand to flight. It was the brave New Englanders, that in 1745, projected the fiege of Louifburg, carried it on with courage, prudence, and unwearied activity, looking up to God to profper the caufe in which they were embarked. Though moft of them never before witneffed a fiege, or even a battle with regular forces, yet they made themfelves mafters of that important fortrefs, and thereby furnifhed Britain, and her allies, with a price to purchafe peace, after a moft difaftrous and unfuccefsful war. This one article, I imagine, fully ballances the account of the New England colonies with the

mother-

mother-country. Though some may pro-
nounce it enthusiasm, I must add, that as
the first planters of New England honoured God, by leaving their estates, their
friends, and their native country, that
they might worship him, though in a wilderness, according to the dictates of their
consciences, God has honoured them and
their posterity with distinguishing instances
of his favour and protection; and often,
when they were on the brink of ruin, has
interposed in their behalf. When they
were but a few men in number, yea, very
few, and strangers in a wilderness , when
by tyranny and persecution, they were dri-
ven from one nation to another, from one
kingdom to another people; God suffer-
ed no man to do them wrong, and re-
proved the numerous tribes of Indians for
their sake. By unusual sickness and mor-
tality, he drove out the heathen, and
planted them, increased his people greatly,
and made them stronger than their enemies. But not to insist on interpositions
of Heaven in their behalf of an older date,

he

he muſt be blind indeed, who cannot per-
ceive evident footſteps of a particular pro-
vidence, in the deſtruction of the formi-
dable ſquadron fitted out againſt them,
1746, under the Duke d'Anville. Pardon
my alſo obſerving the laudable zeal of
the Maſſachuſet's Bay colony, to teſtify
their gratitude to God for the conqueſt of
Canada, by forming plans, and ſubſcribing
large ſums of money for Chriſtianizing the
Indians: plans, that in North Britain,
found not the encouragement they de-
ſerved, and that ſchemes of leſs extenſive
utility, or under a direction leſs to be con-
fided in, have met with, both before and
ſince : plans, that, I am ſorry to add, from
a narrow bigotted ſpirit in South Britain,
were altogether blaſted. In Scotland, carrying money out of the country for ſuch a
purpoſe, was pronounced by many a national loſs ; and a late dignitary of the
church of England is ſaid to have adviſed,
that heathens ſhould rather be permitted
to remain heathens, than to be converted
by Preſbyterians or Congregationaliſts.

D   Whether

Whether the community was moſt ap-
proved of God, that deſired to make the
proper improvement of mercies, or the
community that hindered them from making that improvement, and would not ſuf-
fer them to ſpeak to the Gentiles without
the bounds of their colony, that they might
be ſaved, judge ye.

What if the colonies, unwilling to renounce their claims, and yet afraid of the
calamities of war, ſhould offer to the com-
mander of a fleet, or to the general of an
army, the ſovereignty over them, on con-
dition of turning the arms meant againſt
them to their defence; and ſhould en-
gage, that all the forces ſhould be kept in
pay during life, and lands beſtowed upon
them, that would enable them to live in
greater eaſe and affluence than they would
have done in B—n. How probable would
be the ſucceſs of a temptation, to which
the worldly intereſt of the tempted muſt
ſo ſtrongly incline them?

Or what, if they ſhould throw themſelves into the arms of Holland, Denmark,

or

or fome other Proteftant power, and ob-
tain from them more favourable terms of
fubjection, than ever they afked from their
mother country? Some will fay, thefe are
fchemes that only madmen would adopt.
I allow it. But a jealoufy, however
groundlefs, that thofe who fhould protect
the privileges of a community, are under-
mining them, has often produced fuch
madnefs. By denying them terms, which,
though they are wrong in afking, yet we
can grant with little hurt; we may drive
them into meafures, ruinous both to themfelves and to us, which we might eafily
have prevented, but fhall never be able to
redrefs.

After all, it muft be confeffed probable,
that B—n muft prevail in this difpute with
her colonies. But if fhe prevail by harfh
and fevere meafures, may, if not fow a-
mong them feeds of animofity, which,
when twenty or thirty years have added to
their ftrength, may ripen into a general revolt. I would not intruft my garden to
one, who knew no way to make a tree flou-

D 2   rifh,

rifh, but by lopping off the moft fruitful
branches. I would not intruft my horfe,
or my hounds, to the butcherly phyfician,
who is fond of cutting off a limb, in cafes
where a gentler remedy might be as effectual. A fevere chaftifement may be juftly
inflicted, where it would be neither ho-
nourable nor expedient to inflict it. Fire
and fword are as prepofterous arguments
to teach men allegiance, as to inftruct
them in religion. The taking off the
heads of a faction by capital punifhment,
tends to inflame and enrage their deluded
followers. The friends, the affociates,
the well-wifhers of thofe who immediately
fuffer, conceive, cherifh, and tranfmit to
their pofterity, a rooted averfion to the
men, or to the country, which they confider as the faulty caufe of their fufferings.
A people thus roughly enraged, will foon
find themfelves a method : fury will in
fome cafes fupply the want of prudence,
and mifchief fhall be done in an hour,
which an age fhall hardly repair. Through
unexpected revolutions, bloody meafures
are

are often repaid with ufury, on thofe who advifed them, or who affifted in them. Men only reftrained by fear, will ceafe to fubmit when they find it in their power to rebel, and will eagerly feize the firft opportunity of burfting afunder their galling yoke. From the blood of every individual, who in the field of battle, or on a fcaffold, falls in the American caufe, new enemies to the mother country will fpring up, and in procefs of time, fome foreign power, prompted by hatred or envy to B—n, may affift them to throw off their allegiance. It is only gaining the heart, that deftroys all inclination to revolt. No victories have fuch irrefiftible, happy, and abiding effects, as victories gained by clemency and condefenfion. Princes and ftates have been taught this by fatal experience, who would not be taught it by reafon. The ten tribes would have remained faithful to the houfe of David, had Rehoboam hearkened to the counfel of the old men, to be a fervant unto the people that day, and fpeak good words unto them that they

might

might be his fervants for ever, and to eafe the heavy yoke his father had put upon them. The wholefome feverities of the Duke of Alva, loft Spain the feven United Provinces ; and probably King James II. lived to be convinced, that the bloody Weftern affizes, inftead of eftablifhing his authority, contributed to his ruin. It is to be prefumed, from what has happened in fimilar cafes, that if we give our colonies terms indeed for their intereft, their allegiance will be faithful and perpetual : and if not, that they will renounce it, whenever they can. A fmall matter may now quench the fpark, which, if fuffered to kindle into a flame, may confume all our power and glory.

" But a ftanding army, and the terror " of their vengeance, will reduce Ameri- " cans to their duty, and keep them in " fubjection, without ftroke of fword." I fhall not difpute this, though I think it doubtful. But if open infurrections and rebellions are prevented, fecret difcontent and murmuring increafe. The imports of
                                                    the

the colonies from B—n daily diminish.
A branch of trade, the ballance of which
is about a million per annum in our favour, will be in a great meafure loft;
and our rivals and enemies will fneer, to
fee us facrificing to a trifling point of honour, our moft valuable interefts, as a mer-
cantile nation, and as a naval power.

The ambitious defigns of the houfe of
Bourbon, and their envy and refentment
at the high pinnacle of honour, and the
vaft increafe of territory, acquired by Britain in the late war, cannot allow us to
fpare fuch an army, as will be able to fubdue our colonies, or prevent their revolt,
without expofing our own coafts to the
greateft danger of invafion.

The charge of maintaining fleets and armies fufficient to keep the colonies in fubjection, muft drain Britain of vaft fums of
money, and fo enrich the Americans, as
may in time enable them to attempt the
recovery of their alledged rights, if not
with victory, yet with fuch hurt to Britain,

tain, as all the gain from a conftrained fubjection fhall not compenfate.

An army ftrong enough to awe the wide-extended American continent, feeling their ftrength, might one time or other be feduced by an artful leader, to employ it againft the prince or nation that beftowed it.

It would give me fenfible pain, if in any part of his Majefty's dominions, however remote, Britifh laws and liberties fhould give place to a military government. The precedent would be alarming. It might gradually extend to other colonies, and at laft reach even Britain herfelf.

A ftanding army, the profpect of civil or military preferment, and dread of death to themfelves, and of poverty to their families, may in time fubdue the ftubborn and factious North Americans. Seeing that reft is good, and their land pleafant, like Iffachar, they may bow their fhoulders to bear, without even daring to remonftrate, become fervants to tribute, and tamely fubmit to any ftamp-acts, or hea-

vier

vier burden, that a future G—le fhall im-
pofe upon them. Poffibly too, with fomething of a turbulent fpirit, that cannot be
juftified, they may gradually lofe a fpirit
of liberty. But would that be indeed a benefit to the mother country? Suppofe the
colonies altogether deprived of the power
of taxing themfelves by reprefentatives of
their own chufing, and a military government fully eftablifhed among them; is it
impoffible that a King fhould arife, intoxi-
cated with the fweetnefs, and puffed up
with the pride, of ruling with uncon-
trouled fway fo populous and extenfive a
continent; and ambitious that his will might
give laws in Britain, as well as in North
America? Is it not poffible that North
America, partly ftimulated by revenge,
partly corrupted by mercenary profpects,
fhould offer their fervice, and he accept it,
for reducing us to the fame ftate as themfelves? Is it impoffible. that thofe among
ourfelves, who, from principle or intereft,
prefer an abfolute to a limited monarchy,
and many of the ftanding forces both by

E   fea

fea and land, fhould lend their affiftance for the fame purpofe ?

Some, I know, will fay, that all this is dream and chimera ; but the profpect is not improbable. Defpair fharpens the invention ; and when it cannot find relief, fuggefts a thoufand expedients of revenge. Hard ufage often recoils on them that gave it. Men will think it no crime to return that mifchief upon others, which others unjuftly intended againft them. Nay, men thoroughly enraged, will hurt an enemy, though they cannot do it without hurting themfelves. Samfon is content to die, that he may be avenged of the Philiftines. The commons of Denmark, provoked by the infolence of the nobility, rather than be flaves to their fellow-fubjects, gave up their liberty to their common fovereign, and revenged themfelves of their oppreffois, by fubjecting them to the fame ftate of flavery. Men, enamoured of liberty, when they apprehend it is like to be wrefted fiom them, may, as the laft act of liberty, chufe themfelves a mafter, and
find

find fome confolation in forcing a mafter
upon thofe who have provoked them
Such, therefore, who value their own
freedom, had need to take care how they
drive to extremity the free-born and brave-
fpirited North Americans. Nothing under God can fo much tend to prevent the
eftablifhment of defpotifm in the Biitifh
empire, as every part of that empire con-
fidering it as at once their intereft and duty,
to guard againft encroachments on the
rights of every other part. A large political body is then only healthy and vigorous,
when the whole body feels the diftreffes of
every part, and is reftlefs till they are re-
lieved; and when, if one member fuffers,
all the members fuffer with it. When
any part, efpecially when a more noble and
vital part lofes feeling, it looks as if a mor-
tification was begun, which, if not time-
ly cured, muft end in death. Prudence,
therefore, as well as juftice, obliges the
mother-country to fupport the colonies in
the enjoyment of their natural liberty and
charter-privileges; feeing, if they are en-

E 2   flaved,

flaved, the like fate muft threaten her alfo.

It is fo natural for mankind to defire freedom from controul, and a power of conducting themfelves by their own fentiments and inclinations, without any daring to reftrain or limit them, that he muft be a ftranger to human nature, who thinks that many princes would fcruple to accept abfolute power, when fairly offered it by a number of their fubjects, that could effectually beftow and fupport it.

Britain cannot employ an army, to force the colonies into her meafures, without danger that fuch army may afterwards concur with the colonies in raifing the prince to abfolute monarchy. Self-love in officers and foldiers, will hardly prefer their precarious ftate under parliaments, who, jealous of their liberties, may incline to diminifh or difband them, and think it mighty grievous to allow them half-pay, to the fecurity for the continuance, and probably the increafe of their pay, by beftowing an abfolute power, for the defence of which they

muft

muſt neceſſarily be kept up. It is abſurd to imagine, that men, many of whom are accuſtomed equally to ſneer at religion and patriotiſm, will ſupport the liberty of the people, and the privilege of parliament, with loſs to themſelves, rather than contribute, with a ſolid proſpect of gain to themſelves, to extend the power and prerogatives of the ſovereign.

Should the Americans ſink ſo low, and become ſo thoroughly effeminate, as to be incapable either of helping or hurting us ; ſhould they make no attempt, to do to Britain, as they ſuppoſe Britain has done to them, ſtill their ſituation would furniſh an able and enterprizing miniſter with proper engines for executing the deſigns of an ambitious prince. American offices in the army and in the cuſtoms, beſtowed on electors, on members of parliament, or on thoſe connected with them, would purchaſe for him mercenary troops of the baſeſt ſort, to facilitate his carrying on the moſt deſtructive plans ; men who, in one day, may give liberty more deadly wounds,

than

than fleets or armies, without their aid, could give it in many years.

Say not, that the North Americans are a froward, murmuring people, not to be satisfied. Where were their murmurs, before the unhappy ftamp-act? Where was the corner in his Majefty's dominions, that open rebellion, or fecret difaffection, had lefs difturbed; and where loyalty to the prince, and a zealous, I had almoft faid an enthufiaftic attachment to the mother-country, more univerfally prevailed? Did they ever difpute the right of the Crown to repeal laws enacted in the colonies, and to determine finally in appeals from their courts of juftice; or the right of parliament to regulate their trade and manufactures, fo as they deemed neceffary for the general good of the Britifh empire? Did they not quietly fubmit to prohibitions of carrying, to other nations, commodities that might enable them to interfere with the trade of the mother-country; to prohibitions of manufacturing hats, iron, and fteel; and to many other reftraints, very

preju-

prejudicial to their feparate interefts?
What power of parliament have they ever
queftioned, unlefs the power of levying
taxes, to raife a revenue for the fupport of
government, in America? And fhall we
condemn them without mercy, for quef-
tioning the exiftence of a power, which,
till a few years ago, never appeared?
When were the brave and generous New
Englanders backward, called or uncalled,
to hazard their lives, and fpend their treafure, for the honour and intereft of Britain? Have you forgot their heroic,
though unfuccefsful expeditions againft
Canada; or their furprizing conqueft of
Louifbourg? What had Britain done for
New England before that conqueft, any
way comparable to what New England
then did for Britain? Have not the New
England colonies, on different occafions,
exerted themfelves fo much beyond their
power, that a grateful prince and parliament have feen caufe to refund them?
How ftrong was the connection founded on
fuch a mutual interchange of benefits?

6   Who

Who was the wretched confounder of all this harmony? Who raifed a fpirit of difcord between the mother and children? Children yet unborn will remember his name; but they will remember it with grief and indignation. I will not affert with fome, that when ftate fecrets are revealed, it will appear, that he meant as little friendfhip to Britain as to America; and that the war, dreaded by the Boftonians, was in this fenfe a French war; that it was a war that could only be occafioned through meafures, concerted through French influence. I judge not his intentions. A defire of difcharging the enormous national debt, and the very natural idea, that the colonies ought to bear their proportion of a burden, partly contracted for their benefit, might fuggeft the meafure; and had they been requefted to tax themfelves for fuch a purpofe, their objections againft fubmitting to a parliamentary tax for the fupport of their governors and judges, could not have been a plea againft their complying. Had Mr. G——le been

as

as thoroughly acquainted with the genius
and temper of the North Americans, as
with the ftate of our finances, probably his
demands upon them might have been as
lucrative to us, and to them have appeared equitable and conftitutional. However,
the mother-country has as little reafon as
the colonies to erect ftatues to that Gentle-
man, for fparing the treafure of Britain, at
the expence, at leaft at the hazard, of her
blood.

Whether through miftaken and partial
views of things, or from difhoneft intentions, meafures have been purfued, no
way friendly to the cultivating a good cor-
refpondence between Britain and her colonies, or to the fecuring our religion and
liberties, and his Majefty's facred perfon
and government, againft their chief, I had
almoft faid, their only enemies; what
could tempt a wife and cautious ftatefman
to allow, the bringing upon the carpet,
the affair of fending Bifhops to North America, at a time when the fpirits of many in

that

that continent were fo foured on civil ac-
counts ? Was the flame fo low, that it
needed frefh fuel ? Why, in fo critical a
juncture, was encouragement given to the
negotiations of the epifcopal clergy, for ·
purpofes, to men whofe forefathers had
fled from ecclefiaftic tyranny, utterly odious,
nay, by many of their own denomination,
difapproved ? Did it not look, as if it was
no way difagreeable to fome people, to fee
the colonies ftill further exafperated againft
the parliament, and the parliament againft
them ? Did it not look as if the hand of
fome Joab was fpringing a mine, for divid-
ing a kingdom againft itfelf, in order to its
deftruction ?

A number of melancholy facts in Mr.
Blackburn's very feafonable and interefting
Confiderations on the prefent State of
Popery in Great Britain, partly ftrengthen
fuch fufpicions ; partly demonftrate the
danger of quarrelling at this time with our
fincere friends. For fome years paft,
Popery has mightily increafed in England.

Tares

Tares have been fowed, and fprung up in abundance, while the watchmen, both in church and ftate, have flumbered and flept. Jefuits, banifhed from Popifh countries, for their immoral and treafonable opinions and practices, have found in our Proteftant ifland an undifturbed retreat; and the wifhed-for opportunity of fpreading their poifonous tenets, unobferved, or at leaft not fufficiently checked. It is to be feared, that, when they can venture it with fafety, they may again betake themfelves to affaffinations, maffacres, or gunpowder-plots, the arms with which they have formerly fought for the Catholic caufe. According to their principles, fo noble an end will fanctify the bafeft means, and transfor m, I fhould rather have faid tranfubftantiate, darknefs into light, and evil into good. When fome expreffed their apprehenfions, that offence might be taken at fuch a number of Jefuits retiring into England; they were told, that money was much wanted in the treafury,

and

and that their patrons were too wife to moleft men who brought confiderable fums of it along with them, and placed them in the Englifh funds. The number of Popifh feminaries for the education of Englifh and Irifh children of both fexes, in Flanders, and along the coaft from Boulogne, is truly alarming : efpecially, as many who would pafs for good Proteftants, nay, fome in his Majefty's fervice, fend their children to thefe feminaries. They plead, in excufe, the cheapnefs and goodnefs of the education, and that their religion is not meddled with ; though, in fact, they muft return from them paffionately fond of Popery, and bitterly prejudiced againft the Proteftant faith. At many places in England, as at Bed ley, Edgbafton, and Sedgley, there are large and flourifhing Popifh fchools. In that at Sedgley, there are boarded and educated more than a hundred boys, many of whom are foreigners, who are put out as apprentices to various branches of trade, in which

that

that country is known to excel, efpecially in the manufacture of iron and brafs. In the years 1764 and 1765, large books were publifhed at London and Oxford, to blacken the Reformation and the Reformers, to extol the virtues of Roman Catholics, and to reprefent them as the effect of their religious fentiments. Artful effays were repeatedly inferted in the public News-papers, to folicit a full toleration for a re-ligion, that was now, it feems, become perfectly moderate and harmlefs; fo that Proteftants might folely rely on the ho-nefty and good faith of thofe who profeff-ed it. In the fprings and fummers of thefe years, the difaffected party on the o-ther fide of the water, were particularly active in fending over priefts in difguife, and other emiffaries, and large cargoes of Popifh books, pictures, and other fuch holy lumber. So intolerable was their in-folence, that, not content with quietly en-joying the connivance of government, in fome of our great towns, the fplendid, and

even

even fuperb decorations of Popifh chapels, were fhown to ftrangers among their curiofities. Nay, fome were imprudent enough to let us into the fecret of all this boldnefs, by publifhing, that encouragement was given to hope fo confiderable a mitigation of the penal laws againft Popery, as would almoft prove equivalent to a full toleration. The fucceeding adminiftration, as became good Whigs and Proteftants, gave a confiderable check to the rapid progrefs of thefe evils.

It appears from the reports of Doctors Hyndman, Dick, and Walker, that in many places of the Highlands and iflands of Scotland, Popery has alfo increafed. Had the commiffioners for managing the annexed eftates, erected churches and fchools in the places where they were moft needed, and been careful to fill them with minifters and fchoolmafters, well acquainted with the Popifh controverfy, probably fewer would have been perverted from the Proteftant faith.

Mr.

Mr. Blackburn in his poftfcript, p. 274, mentions fome circumftances, from which it would feem, that the Englifh Papifts are now difpofed to acknowledge the fufpicions of the late Pretender's birth well founded, and to make a pufh, was it in their power, for his Sardinian majefty. To thefe circumftances I would add, that genealogical tables of the houfe of Stuart are faid to be handed about among them, in which the houfe of Hanover are branded as ufurpers, the late Pretender and his two fons are altogether omitted, and the houfe of Savoy is pointed out as entitled by hereditary right to the Britifh crown. This, which can hardly be unknown to his Sardinian majefty, may, perhaps, account for fo wife a prince remaining unactive, whilft the French are engaged in the conqueft of Corfica ; at the utmoft contenting himfelf with remonftrances, perhaps, merely intended to fave appearances : certainly, unlefs feconded by fomething more fpirited than negotiation, not like to have

any

any important effect. Even a remote profpect of the British crown may incline him
to keep well with France, and reſtrain him
from ſuch oppoſition to their encroachments, as good policy would, in other
circumſtances, have dictated. Much more
than this would not be too high a price
for the aſſiſtance of the Bourbon family,
in deſigns againſt our preſent happy eſtab-
liſhment.

If it is true, that ſeveral forts on the
back of our North American colonies are
diſmantled, it muſt be grateful to the Canada Papiſts, thus to open a door for their
haraſſing a ſet of damnable heretics, whom
to ſlay, as they will be taught by the Jeſuits, is to do God good ſervice.

Gentleneſs, not to ſay encouragement
to Jeſuits, and harſhneſs to colonies,
ſteadily attached to Proteſtant principles,
and to the ſucceſſion in the illuſtrious
houſe of Hanover, has an ugly aſpect.
Ye who are now in the adminiſtration,
guard againſt the rocks that have proved

fatal to fome of your predeceffors. Be-
ware of a dangerous ill-grounded confidence in men, who entertain opinions
themfelves, or are under the influence or
direction of fuch as entertain opinions, un-
friendly to our King, our Religion, our
Liberty. When their words are fmoother
than oil, war is in their hearts : though,
therefore, they fpeak fair, believe them
not ; for feven abominations lurk in their
breafts. And O, do not, in rafh and im-
moderate refentment, deprive thofe of the
inclination or ability to help us, whofe
principles are friendly to our beft interefts, and who have been diftinguifhed
for their firm attachment to our revolution fettlement. The happinefs of Britain, and her Colonies, depends, under
God, on their mutual friendfhip. They
can gain little by contending. They may
lofe much.

Let us not be more headftrong in
rufhing upon danger, than the brute cre-
ation. Surely in vain is the net fpread
in the fight of any bird. The prudent

G   man

man forefeeth the evil, and hideth him-felf. It is only the fimple that pafs on and are punifhed.

We read, Judges xxi. 6. " that the " children of Ifrael repented themfelves " for Benjamin their Brother." If Ifrael did well in pitying a Brother, who had fuffered for protecting the moft fhocking and heaven-daring wickednefs, have we not much more caufe to pity, our gene-rous-fpirited and virtuous fellow-fub-jects, the worft crime that can be laid to whofe charge is this, that they have mif-taken, pufhed a little too far, and de-fended in a manner, not the moft refpect-ful to their lawful fuperiors, principles to which we and they are indebted for our civil and our religious liberties.

THE END.

ADVERTISEMENT.

S I N C E fending *thefe fheets to the prefs,*
the Author has feen The State of the Nation, &c. and is happy to find the ideas of
that ingenious performance fo nearly approaching to his own, as to the Americans
taxing themfelves, to pay a certain proportion of the national debt. Though he ap-
prehends, the Colonies will expect little
from a few Reprefentatives in Parliament,
he would flatter himfelf, fome of the commercial advantages propofed to be granted
them, may procure their chearful acqui-
efcence in a meafure, which the prefent
ftate of the Britifh finances *feem to call for.*

CPSIA information can be obtained
at www.ICGtesting.com
Printed in the USA
BVHW011318031121
620448BV00022B/151

9 781379 832904